— THE UNCOMMON —
MILLIONAIRE'S
GUIDE TO FINANCIAL FITNESS

THE UNCOMMON

MILLIONAIRE'S

GUIDE TO FINANCIAL FITNESS

14 Money Lessons Everyone Should Know

ALFRED D. RIDDICK, JR.

Game Time Budgeting, LLC
260 Northland Boulevard, Suite 300
Cincinnati, OH 45246
www.GameTimeBudgeting.com

Cover by Adina Cucicov
Cover photo by Jeff Schaefer Photography
Edited by Shawanda Pauldin
Interior Design by Denis Vorobiov

ISBN: 978-0-9913929-3-3
Printed in the United States of America

Table of Contents

Congratulations for making the decision to take the steps needed to develop a financially fit lifestyle. Today represents the first day of the rest of your financial life, so you should be excited about where you are headed. The journey may not be easy, however, with the proper goals and strategies, you will eventually achieve success because you chose not to quit. You are a winner! Please visit **www.gametimebudgeting.com** (resource page) to download the electronic cash flow planning tools that accompany this workbook.

GOALS

After completing this workbook, you will understand how to:

- Live below (not within) your means
- Give your money better purpose and direction
- Improve cash flow
- Create and follow spending plans
- Develop a renewed money mindset
- Spend your way to debt-free living
- Distinguish between high cost and low cost credit

Three Key Plays

1. On Your Mark, Get Set, Save!
2. Run Your Debt Blitz
3. Get Your Second Wind

The Game Time Budgeting system consists of three simple key plays.

1. It does not matter who you are, at some point in your life something will happen that you did not plan which will cost money to resolve. Since we all know this to be true, you must have an initial emergency fund in place. A good start is $1,000 but that's just the beginning. However, if your income is $25,000 per year or less, $500 should be your initial goal. If you are having trouble keeping your bills paid, $500 or $1,000 may seem like a lot of money right now. As you can see, this workbook consists of many pages. Do not worry, my goal is to walk you through, step-by-step, how to reach your goals.

2. Pay off all debts (excluding primary mortgage). It is difficult to tell you how long this step will take. A number of factors play a role in how quickly you see results. They include: income, debt, and intensity level. Again, you are going to learn exactly what plans to put in place to accomplish this goal. I am sure you would agree that most things in life have been accomplished because someone took the time to make a plan and put the plan into action.

3. While paying off your debt, you will need to continue growing your initial emergency fund. A minimum of 3, 6, or 9 months' worth of living expenses should be in this account. Whichever goal you choose is up to you. My job is to give you the tools to get there.

Money 101

COURSE DESCRIPTION:

Simply stated, money is required to function. Shelter, food, and clothing are basic necessities; each of these cost money. The amount of money you earn is not as important as the amount of money you do not spend. Stop! Read that again. This section is the starting point on your journey to financial fitness. It is designed to establish a foundation for your understanding of personal financial management principles.

OBJECTIVES:

1. To understand commonly used financial terms
2. To understand the effect of taxes on your income
3. To dispel some of the myths you may believe about money

OUTCOMES:

Upon successful completion of this lesson, you will have a better understanding of:
> Common financial terms
> The net effect of federal income tax, state income tax, social security tax and Medicare tax

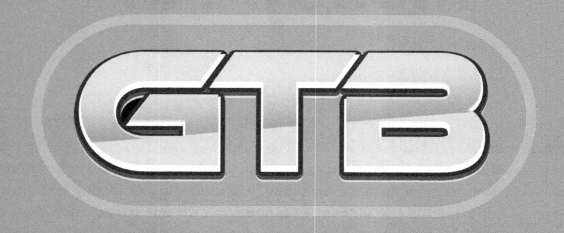

LESSON 1

Your Financial Literacy

A term by any other name may not be the same.

- ➲ Debt
- ➲ Asset
- ➲ Liability
- ➲ Net Worth

- ➲ Interest
- ➲ Term
- ➲ Annual Percentage Rate
- ➲ Co-Sign

- ➲ Overdraft
- ➲ Home Equity

Information is the first key to understanding. Knowledge is the application of information.

The following terms are building blocks for creating a strong financial foundation. There are many more words which could have been included. Keep in mind that learning is a life-long process. If you are given everything, that will make you less likely to seek new information on your own. Having said that, embrace the opportunity to do additional, independent research to become more familiar with the following terms (source: investorwords.com):

1. **Debt** — the amount owed to a person or organization for funds borrowed
2. **Asset** — an item of economic value owned by an individual or corporation that can be converted to cash
3. **Liability** — an obligation that legally binds an individual or company to settle a debt
4. **Net Worth** — total assets minus total liabilities
5. **Interest** — the fee charged by a lender to a borrower for the use of borrowed money, usually expressed as an annual percentage of the principal; the return earned on an investment
6. **Term** — the period of time (e.g., 1, 5, 10 years) during which an agreement is in force
7. **Annual Percentage Rate (APR)** — The yearly cost of borrowing expressed as a percentage
8. **Co-sign** — to sign a promissory note in addition to the borrower and thereby assuming equal liability for it
9. **Overdraft** — the amount by which withdrawals exceed deposits
10. **Home Equity** — the current market value of a home minus the outstanding mortgage balance
11. **Home Equity Line of Credit (HELOC)** — a method of borrowing in which a homeowner may borrow against home equity

Pay Earned vs. Pay Received

- ➔ Salary vs. Hourly Worker
- ➔ Before-Tax Deductions
- ➔ Taxable Income
  - ▸ Federal Withholding

- ▸ FICA
- ▸ Medicare
- ▸ State and City Taxes
- ➔ After-Tax Deductions

The majority of U.S. workers can be classified as salaried or hourly. At different times in your life, you may have been both. Most people would agree that being paid by the hour might be best.

As you may know, your pre-tax deductions for things such as retirement plan contributions, health insurance, disability, and life insurance premiums play a role in determining your net pay. The good part is that you do not pay taxes on this income; however, all deductions affect the amount of money you bring home.

Your federal income tax withholding is based on your income level. The amount deducted from your paycheck depends on schedules produced by the Internal Revenue Service.

Federal Insurance Contributions Act (FICA) is the law which mandates what employees and employers contribute to the nation's Social Security and Medicare programs. Contributions to each program are a specific percentage of gross pay: 6.2% for Social Security and 1.45% for Medicare. This total of 7.65% (6.2% + 1.45%) is paid by the employee along with a matching contribution paid by the employer. Note that "FICA" on your paystub relates to the Social Security portion of the tax only.

Old-Age, Survivor, and Disability Insurance (OASDI) is the official name for social security. Some employers identify social security as OASDI/EE on paystubs. As of 2020, the maximum amount which can be deducted from your pay within one calendar year for social security is $8,537.40 (6.2% X $137,700).

MED/EE (Medicare/Employee) is how many companies identify Medicare contributions on paystubs.

If you live in a state or city that charges income tax, these assessments will be deducted from your paycheck according to the current effective rates.

Depending on your personal preference, you may choose to establish after-tax deductions. These are automatic deductions you determine for things such as a holiday savings or vacation account.

WHERE'S THE MONEY?
Analyzing a paycheck

John B. Free — "Single" salaried employee

❥ Salary: $48,000 per year
❥ Paid once a month: $4,000 per month gross pay

John B. Free is newly employed at Playing to Win, Inc. He is a salaried employee and earns a gross pay of $48,000 each year. Take a walk with John as he uncovers how his $4,000 a month gross pay seems to slowly vanish.

First, let's calculate John's federal tax withholding.

To better understand this, here's a brief note about our federal tax system and how withholding amounts are calculated.

NOTE

The U.S. tax system is based on progressive tax rates. As seen in the following table, all taxpayers pay the same rate on income earned up to certain amounts. For example, if single employee A and single employee B earn $20,000 and $200,000 per year, respectively, each individual would only pay a 10% tax rate on the first $9,700 of income. For this reason, most taxpayers do not have a single tax rate. Each level of income is taxed based on the rate applicable to that income bracket. The calculations are pretty straightforward; however, the IRS issues Publication 15 *(Circular E), Employer's Tax Guide* which includes tables that assist employers in calculating income tax withholding. There are two main methods for calculating withholding taxes: 1) wage bracket method and 2) percentage method. Both methods utilize the progressive tax rates, the employee's filing status, and withholding allowances to determine withholding taxes.

2019 Tax Rates

Tax Rate	Married Filing Jointly	Single
10%	Up to $19,400	Up to $9,700
12%	$19,401 — $78,950	$9,701 — $39,475
22%	$78,951 — $168,400	$39,476 — $84,200
24%	$168,401 — $321,450	$84,201 — $160,725
32%	$321,451 — $408,200	$160,726 — $204,100
35%	$408,201 — $612,350	$204,101 — $510,300
37%	$612,351 or more	$510,301 or more

Source: IRS (head of household and married filing separately intentionally excluded)

Everyone in this country who earns money is supposed to pay income taxes. As John B. Free discovers, his $48,000 a year salary places him in the 22% marginal tax bracket (see 2019 Tax Rates chart). This means his annual salary falls within the income ranges listed on this level and any additional income he receives over $48,000 will be taxed at a rate of 22%. That is, until he reaches the salary cap for the 22% bracket (i.e., $84,200). As you can see in the calculation below, the federal government will take approximately $534.88 ($6,418.50 : 12) of John's money each month.

Something to make you say hmmm...
As mentioned earlier, John's $48,000 per year salary places him in the 22% tax bracket. However, his tax rate is lower.

Here's why. The rates which apply to John's income are:

10% on income up to **$9,700**
12% on income above $9,700 but less than $39,475 ($39,475 − $9,700 = **$29,775)**
22% on income over $39,475 up to $48,000 ($48,000 − 39,475 = **$8,525)**

In this example, John's year-end tax bill would be:

$970.00	(**10%** on **$9,700** of income)
$3,573.00	(**12%** on **$29,775** of income)
+$1,875.50	(**22%** on **$8,525** of income)
$6,418.50	

Based on John's tax bill of $6,418.50, his tax rate as a percentage of his income is **13.37%** ($\frac{\$6,418.50}{\$48,000} \times 100$).

Next, let's calculate John's state tax withholding.

John lives in the state of Ohio; therefore, his state tax withholding is calculated based on the following marginal tax rate chart. Income taxes for your state may be different.

Tax Bracket (Single)	2019 Tax Calculation
$0 — $21,750	0.000%
$21,751 — $43,450	$310.47 + 2.850% of excess over $21,750
$43,450 — $86,900	$928.92 + 3.326% of excess over $43,450
$86,900 — $108,700	$2,374.07 + 3.802% of excess over $86,900
$108,700 — $217,400	$3,202.91 + 4.413% of excess over $108,700
More than $217,400	$7,999.84 + 4.797% of excess over $217,400

Source: Ohio Department of Taxation

Following is the breakdown of how John's monthly state income taxes are calculated based on his gross pay of $48,000 per year.

According to the Ohio tax table above, we must determine the amount of John's income which exceeds $43,450. To do this, use the following formula:

$48,000 (gross pay) – $43,450 = $4,550 (excess over $43,450)

Now, we need to calculate the taxes on this excess amount. To do that, multiply the calculated excess amount times the applicable interest rate for this bracket. In this case:

$4,550 X 3.326% = $151.33

John's year-end state tax liability is determined by adding the tax amount calculated for the excess ($151.33) plus the given tax amount of $928.92 (see chart). This latter figure relates to the tax on the portion of his income less than $43,451. The final tax calculation for the year is:

$151.33 + $928.92 = $1,080.25

Since John is paid once a month, his Ohio taxes are calculated as such:

$1,080.25/12 months = $90.02 per month

Although John has paid income taxes to the federal government ($534.88) and state of Ohio ($90.02), he still has to pay Social Security tax (6.2% of his gross pay) and Medicare tax (1.45% of his gross pay). Please note the calculations shown below.

➲ Social Security Tax = $248 (4,000 x 6.2%)

➲ Medicare = $58.00 ($4,000 x 1.45%)

Social Security tax on your paystub may be represented as FICA (Federal Insurance Contribution Act) or OASDI/EE (Old-age, Survivor, and Disability Insurance/Employee).

SUMMARY

John B. Free — 2019 Monthly Pay

Gross Pay	$4,000.00
Federal Tax	-$534.88
OH State Tax	-$90.02
FICA (Social Security Tax)	-$248.00
Medicare Tax	-$58.00
Net Pay	$3,069.10

How much of John's pay is taken out in taxes?

$$\$534.88 + \$90.02 + \$248.00 + \$58.00 = \textbf{\$930.90}$$

What percentage of John's pay does that number represent?

$$\$930.90 \div \$4,000 = 0.2327$$
$$0.2327 \times 100 = \textbf{23.27\%}$$

After a long month of working, John B. Free finally receives his paycheck. He's shocked by the amount listed in Net Pay. Even though John earns a gross pay of $4,000 a month, he brings home a net pay of $3,069.10. Taxes have consumed $930.90 of his gross pay.

If John lives like he actually brings home $4,000 a month, he is bound to have a long life of using OPM (other people's money) to finance his lifestyle. He needs to learn to live on far less than $36,829.20 in an effort to make his financial dreams come true. This simple example explains how so many people in this country end up in debt. They have not learned how to live on the money they bring home. Living on less than your net pay is crucial if you ever want to develop a wealth building mentality.

By the way, John works almost three months of the year for FREE (kind of). His total taxes due for the year amount to $11,170.80 ($930.90 monthly tax expense x 12 months). That's almost three months' worth of income ($4,000/month x 3 months = $12,000)!

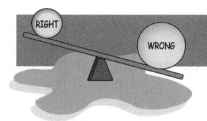

LESSON 3

False Starts

A false start in football occurs when an offensive player (other than the center) moves after he has taken a set position. When this happens, a five yard penalty is assessed against the offense. As with sports, you have to follow the rules of the game with money. If you don't, there is usually a penalty involved. A False Start in the Game Time Budgeting system occurs when you believe something about money that is not true or engage in a behavior that is detrimental to your financial health.

The statements in the list below are common beliefs in many households. On the pages that follow, each False Start is presented and an opposing viewpoint is provided.

- ▸ I *need* my credit card.
- ▸ I deserve _____ so I'm getting it.
- ▸ I have "good" credit.
- ▸ If I could just hit the lottery, all my money problems would be over.
- ▸ It's OK to lend money.
- ▸ It's a good deal.
- ▸ My spouse handles the finances.
- ▸ Debt consolidation programs are a good debt management tool.
- ▸ I can afford it.
- ▸ You'll always have a car payment.
- ▸ Co-signing is a way of helping someone I care about.
- ▸ Cash advances and payday loans help you get through the rough spots.
- ▸ My job is the only way I can get a pay raise.
- ▸ I'm a homeowner.

I *need* my credit card. You don't *need* a credit card. Most people have credit cards because they are more convenient. A debit card can be used in place of a credit card in almost all situations. The main advantage of using a credit card is that you may have some additional security and protection when making a purchase. If you do not pay your credit card balance in full every month, this may be a sign that you are not effectively managing your cash flow.

I deserve _____ so I'm getting it. *Deserve* simply means to merit. You can earn many things in life but when you have the attitude that you deserve something, you can develop the belief that you will do anything to get it (e.g., going into debt to get what you want).

I have "good" credit. The word *good* means something which is advantageous to you or beneficial for you. The word *debt* can be used to replace the word *credit*. If someone lends you something and you have to pay that person back, that's debt. In almost every instance relating to credit, interest is attached to the debt. How many people do you know who have advantageous debt? "Good" credit does not exist, only people who have high, medium, or low credit scores.

If I could just hit the lottery, all my money problems would be over. If you overspend before hitting the lottery, you're probably going to overspend after you hit the lottery. Money only makes you more of what you already are. Too much money can sometimes be more of a headache than not having enough.

It's OK to loan money. Do not ever lend money unless you can accept the possibility that you might not get it back. For example, if you lend money to family members and they do not pay you back, the relationship can become strained. If you truly feel in your heart like helping someone, just give him the money. If you can't afford to do that, then you are probably better off not lending the money.

It's a good deal. Just because something is a good deal does not mean you should buy it. For example, if a new HDTV is on sale for $1,000 from its original price of $2,000, it is only a good deal if you have $1,000 cash and can afford to spend it all on the HDTV.

My spouse handles the finances. When two people get married, they are considered one household. In most marriages, one spouse is usually better than the other at handling financial matters. That is fine; however, discussions still need to take place regarding day-to-day financial affairs. If something were to happen to the spouse who typically manages the finances, then the spouse who has to take responsibility for financial transactions will probably be lost and confused.

Debt consolidation programs are a good debt management tool. Debt consolidation programs rearrange your debt. Instead of paying multiple creditors, these programs allow you to make one payment to a company which in turn sends payments to your individual creditors. Why pay someone to do for you what you can do for yourself? Many people who use debt consolidation programs still do not learn how to manage their money.

I can afford it. *Afford* means being able to financially support the cost of something. Based on this definition, anything you do not have the cash to pay for, you can't afford. Millions of people in this country can't afford things, so there is no need to feel bad. You aren't alone. An entire debt industry was created simply because people could not afford things. Nowadays, people tend to think they can afford something if they can make a monthly payment. Besides a house (and student loans too), how would your life be different if you only bought what you could afford to pay for in cash?

You'll always have a car payment. Please understand that cars are machines that typically decrease in value. They mainly consist of metal, plastic, aluminum, and rubber. If you have to borrow money to buy your car, chances are you can't afford it. Due to the invention of auto leases, many people get to drive around in the car of their dreams. There is one problem; you'll always have a payment. Leasing a car for personal use is similar to renting a car forever.

Co-signing is a way of helping someone I care about. A co-signer is required when a lender views someone as being too great a credit risk. That is why this person has to have a co-signer. In this instance, the lender is not confident the loan will be repaid as agreed. When people co-sign, they are basically telling the lender that they are willing to assume 100% responsibility for the debt if the primary borrower defaults (more than likely they will).

Cash advance stores and payday lenders help you get through the rough spots. Cash advance stores and payday lenders are in business to make a huge profit. They can only make a profit when someone borrows money. You have to ask yourself one question: "If I do not have that extra $100 now, what makes me think I'll have it two weeks from now?" Repeat customers are the real money makers for these types of businesses. The best thing you can do is lower your living expenses, create a spending plan, and stick to it. You could also get a second job to create more cash flow. For a $15 charge on a $100 two-week payday loan, the annual percentage rate is 26 bi-weekly payments $\times$ 15% = 390%. That money is too expensive!

My job is the only way I can get a pay raise. Instead of giving the government an interest free loan every year, adjust your withholding allowances to gain access to your money throughout the year. If you have a skill or talent, market it for money. Improve your cash flow by lowering your living expenses. Have a yard sale. You get the idea.

I'm a homeowner. Unless you have a satisfaction of mortgage document in your possession or live in a home that was paid for before you inherited it, you do not own a home. You simply have control over the home that your lender owns.

Owning a house gives you a tax advantage. If you keep paying your lender as agreed in your mortgage terms, you will eventually own your home. It just might take you 15, 20, or 30 years. Regarding your house giving you a tax advantage, carefully review the following illustration.

Mortgage Amount	Multiplied by:	Interest Rate	Equals	Yearly Interest Paid
$100,000	x	5%	=	$5,000

Taxable Income	Multiplied by:	Tax bracket	Equals	Yearly Taxes Paid
$5,000	x	22%	=	$1,100

The above example is based on a character named John B. Free. His base salary is $48,000 a year; therefore, he's in the 22% tax bracket. If his mortgage was paid off, he could no longer deduct the mortgage interest. In this instance, his taxable income would increase by $5,000.

Like most people, John is excited over giving his lender $5,000 in mortgage interest to avoid giving the IRS $1,100 in taxes if his home was paid off. A paid-for house means you can no longer write off mortgage interest; therefore, your taxable income will be higher. For your sanity, reread the previous false start and review the chart.

Some people might say a house, for example, is nothing more than a lifestyle choice. When you look at the various costs (homeowner's insurance, real estate taxes, maintenance and repairs) involved, it is a very expensive purchase. Besides, the only way to get money out of your house is to sell it for more than you owe or borrow against the equity which puts you back into debt.

LESSON 4

Ways To Save

- ⊜ Bundle services (internet, cable, phone)
- ⊜ Use coupons
- ⊜ Pack your lunch
- ⊜ Enjoy FREE entertainment
- ⊜ Decrease hair and nail appointments
- ⊜ Comparison shop (e.g., insurance)
- ⊜ Make gifts
- ⊜ Shop thrift stores
- ⊜ Wash clothes instead of dry cleaning
- ⊜ Vacation off-peak
- ⊜ Adjust thermostat settings
- ⊜ Cancel subscriptions
- ⊜ Create a spending plan
- ⊜ Use tax refund wisely

There are numerous ways in which to save money. No matter what options you choose, the end result has to be an increase in available cash. Keep in mind there are only two ways to increase cash flow in your home:

1. decrease living expenses
2. increase income (second or part-time job)

If there were other legal avenues, they would have been discovered by now.

One of the ways to increase cash flow in your home is to minimize living expenses. The list above contains only a few suggestions. There are other areas in which you can reduce your cost of living and save money.

Take a moment to locate a blank sheet of paper or open the notes app in your smartphone. As an exercise, think about your respective household and spending habits. Give yourself three minutes to write down as many ways as you can think of to save money.

Congratulations! You're on your way to increasing your cash flow.

L E S S O N 5

Couples and Money

Money is one of the leading causes of arguments among couples. Let's face it, it is not a sexy topic. Each of us thinks a certain way about personal finance and tend to think we are 100% correct. Wrong! There is your way, my way, and our way. You may have more fun in your relationship if you concentrate on our way.

Like most people, much of what you believe and feel about money was formed early in your childhood. Who is to say what is right or wrong when most of the time you do the things you do because that is the way you have always done them. Rarely do you ever pause and say to yourself, *Why*?

Here are a few questions that might help you and your significant other have more meaningful conversations about money:

1. What does money mean to you?

2. What role does money play in your life today and how, if at all, do you want that role to change in the future?

3. How would you describe our system with money?

4. What are your thoughts on how we could improve our money system as a couple? (Hint: No *I* or *you* statements, only *we*)

5. If you had to list our top three financial values as a couple, what would they be?

6. What major purchases do you see us making in the next 12 to 18 months?

7. What would you like to be able to do with our money that we are not doing now?

8. In what areas of our financial system do you think we should be spending less money?

9. What one financial accomplishment would you be most proud of if we were able to achieve it as a couple?

10. When we hit some of our financial goals, how would you like to celebrate?

11. How do you see us living after we retire?

If you and your significant other did not discuss the previous questions, stop reading now and schedule a time to complete this assignment. Remember, your money will not show itself how to behave better; only you two have the power to do that. So get to work!

Three Options for Handling Money as a Couple

Finding that one person out of the billions of people on earth that you want to spend the rest of your life with is not that easy. Determining how you want to handle money can be just as challenging for some couples. However, there are usually only three options to consider:

Option 1: Together

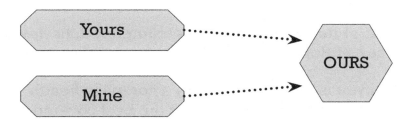

Option 2: Separate

Option 3: Hybrid (Joint and Separate)

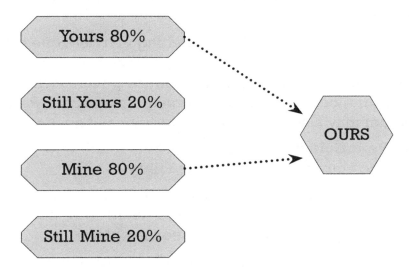

If you are in a long-term relationship, it would be wise to look at your partner's credit report and know his or her credit score. It is a simple case of I'll show you mine if you show me yours. If this individual is hesitant, that does not necessarily mean something is being hidden. However, I do believe getting financially naked is a good idea before exchanging wedding vows. Whatever you discover during this process will create great conversation starters and allow you to better understand your future spouse's financial history.

After you get married, here's a list of items that should be completed, however the research can begin before you say, "I do!"

- **Health Insurance** — If each of you is being covered by a company health plan, determine which of your respective plans provides the best coverage for married couples and at the lowest cost. Because marriage is a life changing event, most companies allow you to make adjustments to your health plan outside of open enrollment dates.

- **Life Insurance** — After marriage, some couples decide to take on bigger expenses in the form of a larger home or more expensive cars now that their incomes are combined. It is not uncommon for someone in the relationship or both individuals to have a child or two. Life insurance is a way of protecting income so that the remaining family members can survive. Whomever you meet with to discuss your life insurance needs, please be sure you fully understand (pros and cons) of each type of policy that is presented. Steer clear of anyone who seems too anxious to sell a policy and not concerned about understanding your needs.

- **Auto Insurance** — Including both cars, if applicable, on the same policy may allow for a multi-car discount.

- **Homeowner's or Renter's Insurance** — Even before getting married, one of you may already have a home or apartment. Carrying the proper insurance can protect your assets. If you have your homeowner's or renter's insurance policies with the same company as your auto insurance, you may be eligible for a discount. Paying your premiums in one lump sum may also qualify for an additional discount.

- **Establish Your Spouse as a Beneficiary** — For any accounts relating to your estate, most likely you will name your spouse as a beneficiary.

- **Create or Amend Your Will** — Documenting your final wishes is a great way to show others how much you care. Creating a living will and health care power of attorney are also great ways to prepare for any unforeseen events.

- **Modify your Withholding** — Upon your return to work after getting married, be sure to change your W-4 form to ensure the correct amount of taxes are taken out of your paycheck. The next time you file your taxes, decide if you will now change your status to married filing jointly (more common) or separately.

The assignments for Quarter 1 are listed below. The Game Time Budgeting electronic cash flow tools will be used to complete some of these exercises.

Creating S.M.A.R.T. Financial Goals

What Do You Really Earn?

Draft Night — monthly income snapshot

Net Worth Calculation

You and Your Money

BANKING ACCOUNT TIP

Consider creating Payable On Death bank accounts if you do not currently have them. A Payable On Death (POD) account is a regular bank account that names a specific person as the beneficiary of your money once you (the bank account holder) die. To set up this type of account notify your bank of the legal name of the person you want to inherit the money. In this one simple step, you avoid probate court and ensure that your loved one will receive the money he or she is due.

Some banks or credit unions may require the POD beneficiary to submit a copy of his ID and provide a signature. You should not have to incur any fees to do this. If you are charged, are you banking with the wrong institution?

Creating S.M.A.R.T. Financial Goals

Specific
Measurable
Actionable
Realistic
Time Specific

This is an example of a S.M.A.R.T. goal:

I will save $50 a month for the next 12 months beginning February 1 of this year by creating a spending plan and living by that spending plan.

Short Term Goals (present to one year)

_____
_____
_____
_____
_____
_____
_____

Long Term Goals (more than one year from now)

_____
_____
_____
_____
_____
_____

What Do You Really Earn?

Based on your Gross Wages per pay period, calculate the percent deducted for each category.

Name

Pay Period

Income			
	Gross Pay		
Deductions			% of Gross Pay[1]
Taxes	Federal Income Tax		
	Social Security Tax		
	Medicare Tax		
	State Tax		
	City Tax		
Other Deductions	401 (k)		
	Medical Benefits		
	Disability		
	Other_____		
	Other_____		
	Other_____		
	Other_____		
	Other_____		
** Total Net Pay **			

Based on this amount, what is your annual take-home pay? _____

This is the number you have to work with to make all your financial dreams come true.

[1]Deduction amount ÷ gross pay × 100.

Draft Night

When players are drafted, they receive a certain amount of money as compensation for the service they provide. This form represents a snapshot of your "monthly" income plus cash on hand. **Fill in the appropriate amounts using a recent check stub and bank account statements.**

INCOME	
Gross Monthly Income	
Alimony	
Child Support	
Other	
Total Gross Income	

BEFORE-TAX DEDUCTIONS	
Dental Plan	
Healthcare Reimbursement	
Medical Plan	
Retirement Savings Plans	
Total Deductions	

AFTER-TAX DEDUCTIONS	
Total Deductions	

TAXES	
Federal Taxes	
State Taxes	
Social Security (OASDI)	
Medicare (MED/EE)	
City Taxes	
Total Taxes	

NET PAY	

CURRENT SAVINGS	
Account #1 Balance (his)	
Account #2 Balance (hers)	
Account #3 Balance (joint)	
Total Savings	

CURRENT CHECKING	
Account #1 Balance (his)	
Account #2 Balance (hers)	
Account #3 Balance (joint)	
Total Checking	

Net Worth Calculation

This worksheet will help you calculate your net worth. Net Worth is determined by subtracting your Liabilities (what you owe) from your Assets (what you own). Enter the current value (how much something is worth today) in the appropriate column. Amounts listed in the "Debt Owed" column should be the payoff balance for that respective line item. (Visit www.kbb.com to calculate a current market value for your automobiles.)

ASSETS

Item/Description	Current Value	-	Debt Owed	=	Equity
Home #1					
Home #2					
Car #1					
Car #2					
Cash					
Checking #1					
Checking #2					
Savings					
Brokerage Account					
Retirement Plan #1					
Retirement Plan #2					
Other:					
Other:					
Other:					
Other:					
			Total Assets		

sum "Equity" column

LIABILITIES

	Debt Owed
Credit Card Debt	
School Loan	
Medical Bills	
Other:	
Other:	
Other:	
Total Liabilities	

sum "Debt Owed" column

NET WORTH

NET WORTH	=	TOTAL ASSETS	-	TOTAL LIABILITIES

Discussion Topics:

1. Is your net worth what you thought it would be? Explain

2. How is net worth impacted after deducting your effective tax rate from pre-tax account balances (e.g., 401K)?

3. What would your net worth be if you had no liabilities (DEBT-FREE)?

You and Your Money

The following questions will help guide you toward uncovering the root cause of your financial behaviors.

1. What were you taught about money as a child?

    _____

    _____

    _____

    _____

2. How would you describe your current financial situation?

    _____

    _____

    _____

    _____

3. What does money mean to you?

    _____

    _____

    _____

    _____

4. Describe the process by which you handle your household finances after payday.

    _____

    _____

    _____

5. How do you determine why and when to spend money?

    _____

    _____

    _____

    _____

6. What is preventing you from saving more money?

_____

_____

_____

_____

7. What do you think of when you hear the word budget?

_____

_____

_____

_____

8. If you had a $1,000, $2,500, or $5,000 emergency tomorrow, how would you handle it?

_____

_____

_____

_____

QUARTER 2

Credit and Forms of Debt

COURSE DESCRIPTION:

Credit, by definition, is the contractual agreement by which a borrower receives something of value now and agrees to repay the lender at a later date (source: investorwords.com). There are many dimensions to credit; however, a more complete understanding will be gained by focusing on the topics presented in this section. You will also begin to analyze your personal debt.

OBJECTIVES:

1. To understand the players in the credit game
2. To understand the various types of credit
3. To understand credit management
4. To understand credit reporting
5. To understand where and to whom you owe debt

OUTCOMES:

Upon successful completion of this lesson, you will have a better understanding of:

> How the credit market works
> What types of credit you have and the pros/cons of each
> What actions positively and negatively impact your credit score
> The various credit reporting bureaus
> Debt-to-income ratios

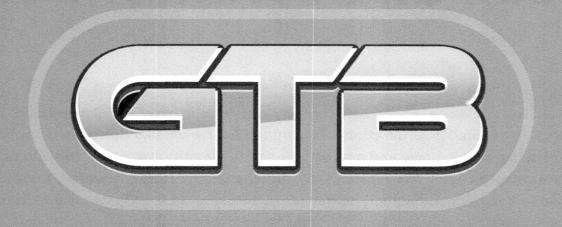

LESSON 6

Players in the Credit Game

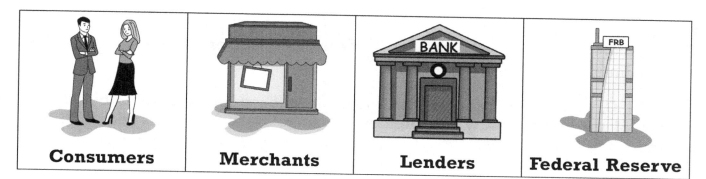

| Consumers | Merchants | Lenders | Federal Reserve |

Consumers use credit to buy things that cost more than they are willing or able to purchase with their available cash. For example, many people use credit to buy a house, car, or pay for an education.

Merchants are retailers which buy items at wholesale prices and sell them at retail prices (e.g., Wal-Mart, Target). Retailers are charged a merchant service fee by credit card issuers for each credit transaction.

Lenders are private or public entities (e.g., banks or credit unions) which make funds available for others to borrow. They act as a link between the consumer and the merchant.

Federal Reserve is the government's bank because it maintains the U.S. Treasury's account, facilitates the collection of federal taxes, and issues and redeems treasury securities. The Federal Open Market Committee (FOMC) regulates the amount of money and credit that is available for the economy.

Pop Quiz

1. What is used to make U.S. paper currency?

_____

_____

2. What department within the U.S. Treasury is responsible for manufacturing paper money? Coins?

_____

_____

LESSON 7

Types of Credit

- ➡ Secured Credit
- ➡ Unsecured Credit
- ➡ Installment Credit
- ➡ Revolving Credit
- ➡ Non-Installment Credit

Secured Credit is any debt or loan which is backed by collateral (borrower's pledge of specific property to a lender to secure repayment of a loan). If you are thinking about houses, cars, and boats as examples of secured credit, you are exactly right. If you stop paying your lender, the pledged property will be seized. Remember, it is not your property until it is paid for.

Unsecured Credit is the opposite of secured credit. It is not backed by collateral. Unsecured credit is given based on your credit history or credit score. Credit cards are a good example of unsecured credit. Personal loans and bank overdrafts also qualify as unsecured credit. From a lender's perspective, the advantage of issuing unsecured credit is that the annual percentage rate charged is usually more profitable than secured credit. From a borrower's perspective, the disadvantage is that you may be provided with money to buy items which you can't afford to repay.

Installment Credit has a fixed number of payments and can be secured or unsecured. Examples include mortgages, auto loans, boat loans, student loans, personal loans, home equity loans and vacation loans. The main advantage of this type of credit is that the payment is usually the same amount month after month until the debt is repaid. The disadvantage is that the payments are due in full each month even if you don't have an income as in the case of a job loss.

Revolving Credit is a type of credit that does not have a fixed number of payments. As you make a minimum payment, credit is always available assuming you have not reached your credit limit. Credit cards are a good example of revolving credit. They can be classified as two types of credit: unsecured and revolving. The main disadvantage of using credit cards is spending more money than you can repay when the bill is due.

Non-Installment Credit is any type of loan which must be repaid in full by a specific date. Examples include electric bill, garbage collection bill, water bill, and phone bill. The main advantage is a creditor allows a consumer to use their services when needed and sends a bill at a later date for the total amount due.

LESSON 8
Credit Management

What is a FICO score?

FICO scores are used to determine an individual's credit worthiness. Scores range from 300 to 850.

FICO score range	Rating
More than 750	Excellent
700 to 749	Good
650 to 699	Fair
Less than 650	Poor

From a lender's point of view, the higher your credit score, the lower the risk of you defaulting on a loan (debt). In contrast, the lower your credit score, the higher the risk you will default on your debts. Thus, the interest rate charged on your debt is higher.

Millions of people in this country are fascinated with their FICO score. Unfortunately, most people do not really understand what it represents or how the love affair began with these four letters. Here are a few interesting points regarding FICO:

- In 1956, Bill Fair (engineer) and Earl Isaac (mathematician) founded Fair Isaac and Company with an initial investment of $400 each.
- The company name changed to Fair Isaac Corporation in 2003.
- Fair Isaac Corporation became FICO in 2009.
- FICO employs about 3,400 people worldwide. FICO had approximately $1.16 billion in revenue during 2019.

Anatomy of a FICO score

35% Payment History
30% Debt
15% Length of Credit History
10% New Credit
<u>10% Types of Credit</u>
FICO Score

Payment History

Because payment history carries the most weight when calculating a credit score, the worst thing you can do is pay your bills late or not at all. As you can guess, non-payment and/or late payment of bills lowers your credit score the most. Your payment history includes:

- Payment information on different types of credit accounts (secured, unsecured, revolving, installment)
- Public records and collections (e.g., liens, foreclosures, bankruptcies)
- Delinquency details (e.g., 30, 60, 90 days late)
- Number of accounts not showing late payments

The primary components of the remaining categories are listed below:

Debt

- How much is owed on various accounts
- Balances on certain types of accounts. As senseless as it may be, having a small balance on a credit account may be better than having a zero balance. The credit reporting bureaus may view you as being someone who "manages credit wisely."
- Number of accounts which have balances
- How much credit is being used (utilization rate = credit used/credit line). For example, if you have a credit card with a $1,000 limit and you have used $100, your utilization rate is 10% ($100/$1,000).

Length of Credit History

- How long credit accounts have been active
- How long it's been since the account's most recent action

New Credit

- Recent requests/inquiries for credit within the past 12 months; Ordering a credit report from a credit reporting agency has no effect on your score. Sometimes lenders request credit scores to they can send a "pre-approved" offer in the mail. These inquiries aren't counted in your score either

Types of Credit

- Credit types take into consideration your mix of various accounts (e.g., revolving, merchant, installment).
- Types of credit represent the different kinds of credit you have and how much of each is being used.

Ways to raise your score

- ◆ Pay bills on time
- ◆ If you've missed payments, get current and stay current
- ◆ Pay off a collection amount
- ◆ Negotiate an easier payment schedule
- ◆ Keep balances low on credit cards (a zero balance is ideal)
- ◆ Pay off debt rather than moving it around
- ◆ Do not open credit accounts you don't need
- ◆ Request some good will from your creditor. In writing, ask the lender to remove negative information such as a late payment from your credit history if you have paid consistently.

Just for fun, it would be interesting if the following information were also used to determine credit scores:

- ◆ percentage of income saved or invested
- ◆ debt-to-income ratios
- ◆ how much money you currently have in savings
- ◆ whether or not you have at least 6 months of living expenses in your emergency fund
- ◆ net worth at your current age as compared to others in your same age group and income level

LESSON 9
Credit Reporting .

Obtaining a Credit Report

Here are the most common credit reporting bureaus.

Credit Reporting Agency	Credit Score Name	Website	Phone
Equifax	BEACON® Score	www.equifax.com	800-685-1111
Experian	Experian/Fair Isaac Risk Model	www.experian.com	888-397-3742
TransUnion	EMPIRICA®	www.transunion.com	800-888-4213

The Fair and Accurate Credit Transactions Act gives consumers the right to a FREE copy of their credit report from each of the "big three" once within a 12-month cycle. To obtain a FREE copy of your credit report, do one of the following:

1. Visit www.annualcreditreport.com
2. Call 1-877-322-8228
3. Complete the **Annual Credit Report Request Form:**
   www.consumer.ftc.gov/articles/pdf-0093-annual-report-request-form.pdf
   Once the form is completed, mail it to:
   > Annual Credit Report Request Service
   > P.O. Box 105281
   > Atlanta, GA 30348-5281

Your credit score may be different at each of the above agencies due to various reporting methods.

If you would like to know more about the government's role in protecting consumers, please visit the Federal Trade Commission website: *www.ftc.gov*.

Credit Report Errors

The Fair Credit Reporting Act discusses procedures for correcting mistakes on your credit report.

- ➲ Alert the appropriate credit bureau in writing.
- ➲ Specifically describe the mistakes and provide proof (copies of appropriate documents — NOT originals).

- Write the creditor as well. Describe the reporting error and provide proof to support your claim. Insist they copy you on correspondence with the credit bureau.
- The credit bureau should resolve your issue within 30 days.
- Send your letter(s) certified mail with return receipt requested to have proof they were received.

This sample letter can be used after you have discovered an error on your credit report.

Date
Your Name
Your Address
Your City, State, Zip Code

Complaint Department
Name of Credit Bureau
Address
City, State, Zip Code

Dear _____:

Information contained in the attached credit report is inaccurate. I have circled the disputed line items accordingly. In particular (identify item(s) disputed by name of source, such as creditors or tax court, and identify type of item, such as credit account, judgment, etc.) is (inaccurate or incomplete) because (describe what is inaccurate or incomplete and why). I am requesting the item be deleted (or request another specific change) to maintain the accuracy of my credit file.

Enclosed are copies of (use this sentence if applicable and describe any enclosed documentation, such as payment records, court documents) which offer validity to my stated concerns. Please investigate (this or these) matter(s) and (delete or correct) the disputed item(s) as soon as possible.

I expect a written response within a 30-day period according to the provisions stated in the Federal Fair Credit Reporting Act. I can be reached at ___-___-___ if you have questions.

Sincerely,

Your Name

Enclosures: (List what you are enclosing)

Is a card just a card?

Charge Card

A plastic card in which the balance is payable in full each month; no periodic or annual percentage rate

Credit Card

A plastic card which carries a revolving balance for a small fee (i.e., interest); minimal payment required

Debit/Check Card

A plastic *card* issued by a bank which allows bank clients access to their account to withdraw cash or pay for goods and services

Did you ever think a credit card was the same as a charge card? Out of the three cards listed above, you must have cash in the bank to use a debit/check card. It makes you wonder why the others are so popular.

DEBIT/CREDIT CARD LOSS TIP

If you have reason to believe your debit card has been lost or stolen, call the card issuer immediately. Your liability for unauthorized use of your ATM or debit card can get expensive, depending on how quickly you report the loss.

Here are a few items to remember from the Electronic Funds Transfer Act:

❷ If you report your debit card lost or missing before it is used, you are not responsible for any unauthorized withdrawals.

❷ If you report the loss within two business days after you realize your debit card is missing, your liability is limited to $50. If you report the loss after two days but before 60 days, your liability is limited to $500.

❷ If you do not report unauthorized use of your debit card 60 days after your bank mails the statement documenting the unauthorized use, it is possible you could lose all the money in your bank account.

If you have reason to believe your *credit card* has been lost or stolen, under the Fair Credit Billing Act (FCBA), your liability for unauthorized use tops out at $50. However, if you report the loss before your credit card is used, the FCBA states that you are not responsible for any charges you did not authorize. If your credit card number is stolen, but not the card, you are not liable for unauthorized use.

Always check the policies of your card issuer.

THE HISTORY OF CREDIT CARDS

1950 — The Diners Club card was created by Frank McNamara and his business partner Ralph Schneider. The idea for the first charge card resulted from a meal at New York's Major's Cabin Grill in 1949. Frank McNamara had finished dinner and when the bill arrived, he realized he had forgotten his wallet. His wife rescued him and took care of the bill. Not surprisingly, McNamara decided never to be in such a dilemma again. In February 1950, he and his partner, Schneider, returned to Major's Cabin Grill. This time, McNamara paid the bill with a small, cardboard card. The Diners Club card claims to hold the title of the first credit card in widespread use.

1959 — American Express introduced plastic cards primarily used for travel and entertainment.

1966 — Birth of the general purpose credit card (what most people use today) by Bank of America. The rest, as they say, is history.

Point of interest

In 1968, U.S. credit card debt was approximately $2 billion. At the end of 2019, it was approximately $1.098 trillion (source: Federal Reserve).

Understanding Your Debt

This list is your first step toward a lifelong habit of giving your money purpose and direction. Using these worksheets can help you create a monthly spending plan and better prepare you for the Debt Blitz process. You will use the **Game Time Budgeting electronic cash flow planning tools** to complete these exercises. If you do not have the capability to use the Game Time Budgeting electronic cash flow planning tools, here is your chance to reintroduce yourself to using a calculator.

Starting Line — bill due dates ☐

Personal Fouls — list of debts ☐

Bench Warmer — emergency fund target ☐

Trick Plays — non-monthly bills/expenses ☐

Starting Line (see Game Time Budgeting electronic cash flow planning tools)

Because most people have a number of items which require payment on a monthly basis, it is best to determine the exact amount due and a specific due date. By completing this activity, you will begin to see your financial situation in a much clearer light. This is a simple exercise, but very powerful because it provides more structure to your personal finances. Please take the opportunity to complete your **Starting Line** worksheet. All you have to do is enter your monthly bills and the specific date they are due.

Personal Fouls (see Game Time Budgeting electronic cash flow planning tools)

Next, you need to learn more about your cash flow. To do this, you have to understand who is financing your debt, your monthly debt payments, and how much money is needed to pay off your debt in full. In the Game Time Budgeting system, this exercise is called **Personal Fouls.**

Bench Warmer (see Game Time Budgeting electronic cash flow planning tools)

Some emergencies are bigger than others. Having at least 3 to 9 months of mandatory living expenses in your emergency fund is a good idea. Game Time Budgeting calls these cash reserves *Bench Warmers*. When determining how much money you need in your emergency fund, pretend you know you are going to get laid off in three months. What "mandatory expenses" (e.g., shelter, food, transportation, utilities, medication) have to be paid? Subscriptions to magazines, dinners at restaurants, and vacations do not make the list. Once you have an idea of how much money is needed to support your necessities for a month, it is easy to multiply that number by 3, 6, or 9 to determine how much you need in your fully funded emergency reserve. Keep in mind that this will be a very large number. Saving this amount in cash will not happen overnight, but at least you know what number to aim for.

Remember, the first key play of the Game Time Budgeting system is On Your Mark, Get Set, Save! A good starting goal could be $500, $1,000, or even $1,500. After you have learned how to incorporate saving into your lifestyle, do not stop. Continue to deposit money into this fund since you can't guess how expensive your next emergency will be.

Trick Plays — Non-Monthly Payments (see Game Time Budgeting electronic cash flow planning tools)

Have you ever received a bill you had forgotten was coming? It has happened to almost everyone at some point in their lives. These unexpected bills can have a tremendous impact. The Game Time Budgeting system refers to these surprises as *Trick Plays*. The examples below present some of the bills or expenses you may experience on an irregular or non-monthly basis. If you can think of something else, add it to this list and insert it on your **Trick Plays** worksheet. This is your workbook, so write in it as much as you wish.

- ➔ Real Estate Taxes (non-escrow)
- ➔ Homeowner's Insurance (non-escrow)
- ➔ Auto Insurance
- ➔ Homeowner's Association Fees
- ➔ Auto Registration
- ➔ Garbage and Recycling
- ➔ School Uniforms
- ➔ Christmas Gifts
- ➔ Birthday Celebrations

To better assist with planning for these surprises, it is best to sit down and take a good look at your non-monthly or irregular expenses. To do this, simply determine how much money is needed to cover the cost of that item for one full year. For example, if you know your homeowner's insurance is $900 and it is due once a year, convert that amount to a monthly bill ($900/12 months = $75 per month). When creating your monthly spending plan, you would save $75 a month until you have the entire $900. Depending on your comfort level, you could put this money in an envelope or deposit it in the bank. Be sure to keep track of where the money is and its purpose.

Here is another example: If you know you need $240 six months from now, you would use this equation: $240/6 months = $40 per month. You would now add $40 a month into your spending plan. At the end of six months, you will have the entire $240 with no major impact on your budget.

Starting Line

If you have ever seen a track meet, each runner has to begin his race at the starting line. When organizing your personal finances, you have to start at the beginning. The good thing about this race is that it is not over until you have won. It does not matter how long it takes you to finish. You also should not worry about the competition. **This worksheet shows monthly payments and due dates for all your bills. For items that have a fluctuating monthly payment (e.g., water or electricity), please enter an average monthly payment amount and due date.**

Debt	Monthly Payment	Due Date
First Mortgage		
Second Mortgage		
Homeowner Association Fee		
Car Payment #1		
Car Payment #2		
Car Payment #3		
Auto Insurance		
Student Loan #1		
Student Loan #2		
Electricity		
Water		
Gas		
Bundle (phone, cable, internet)		
Phone		
Cable		
Internet		
Garbage & Recycling		
Alarm		
Health Insurance		
Doctor Bills		
Medications		
Child Care		
Disability Insurance		
Life Insurance		

Personal fouls are called in basketball when one player displays unsportsmanlike behavior toward another. Regarding your finances, the bad conduct is being performed by debt against you. **Enter the name of your creditor in the "Financed by" category. Next, enter the interest rate, monthly payment and payoff amount on that respective debt. To calculate the ratio, enter your monthly <u>net pay</u> and sum of all monthly debt (payments). Debt-to-income ratio = (Total Monthly Debt/Monthly Net Pay) X 100.**

Mortgage	Financed by	Interest Rate (%)	Monthly Payment	Payoff Amount
First Mortgage				
Second Mortgage				
Total				

Automobiles	Financed by	Interest Rate (%)	Monthly Payment	Payoff Amount
Car Payment #1				
Car Payment #2				
Car Payment #3				
Total				

School Loans	Lender	Interest Rate (%)	Monthly Payment	Payoff Amount
Student Loan #1				
Student Loan #2				
Total				

Credit Cards	Lender	Interest Rate (%)	Monthly Payment	Payoff Amount
Total				

Other	Lender	Interest Rate (%)	Monthly Payment	Payoff Amount
Total				

Your debt to income ratio represents the percentage of your net pay used to fund your debt payments.

Debt-to-Income Ratio:

Monthly Net Pay:

Total Monthly Debt:

Debt to Income Ratio:

How financially fit are you?

Less than 36%	Manageable
37 - 42%	Borderline
43 - 49%	At Risk
50% or Higher	Get help NOW!

Gross pay is normally used to calculate a debt-to-income ratio. Net pay was intentionally chosen to provide a more accurate picture.

Bench Warmers

Bench warmers or second string players are placed on a team to be used as reserves. **This form is designed to show exactly how much money you need in "reserve" to survive each month, especially in the case of an interruption of income. This is a starting point on your road to having 3 to 9 months of expenses in reserve. For each category, enter the average amount spent per month.**

EXPENSES		Monthly Total
Housing	1st Mortgage	
	2nd Mortgage	
	Rent	
Utilities	Electricity	
	Water	
	Gas	
	Phone	
	Garbage and Recycling	
Necessities	Food	
Transportation	Car Payment #1	
	Car Payment #2	
	Gas & Oil	
	Insurance #1	
	Insurance #2	
Personal	Disability Ins.	
	Health Ins.	
	Life Ins.	
	Child care	
Total Monthly Necessities		
3 months of living expenses		
6 months of living expenses		
9 months of living expenses		

Trick Plays!

During a game, some teams implement trick plays to catch their opponent off guard. Some of your bills occur once every three months (e.g., insurance) or maybe twice a year (e.g., real estate taxes). Unfortunately, these bills tend to sneak up on you at the worst possible moment. **These items should be annualized and converted to monthly budget line items. By doing this, the money can be saved each month and prevent you from blowing your budget by being caught off guard. Enter the annual cost for the applicable items in the "Annual Amount" column. To determine the monthly budget expense, simply divide the annual cost by 12.**

ITEM	ANNUAL AMOUNT		MONTHLY AMOUNT
Real Estate Taxes		/ 12 =	
Homeowner's Insurance		/ 12 =	
Garbage & Recycling		/ 12 =	
Auto Insurance		/ 12 =	
Auto Replacement		/ 12 =	
Auto Repairs		/ 12 =	
Life Insurance		/ 12 =	
Appliance Replacement		/ 12 =	
Disability Insurance		/ 12 =	
Dental Work		/ 12 =	
Medical Bills		/ 12 =	
IRS (Self Employed)		/ 12 =	
Tuition		/ 12 =	
Vacation		/ 12=	
Gifts (Christmas Included)		/ 12 =	
Homeowner's Association Fees		/ 12=	
Veterinary Bills		/ 12=	
		/ 12=	
		/ 12=	
		/ 12=	
		/ 12=	
		/ 12=	
		/ 12=	

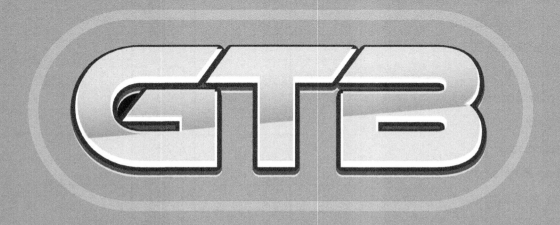

Your Financial Fitness

COURSE DESCRIPTION:

The information learned in the Money 101, Credit and Forms of Debt sections has prepared you to take the next step regarding your personal finances. By this time, you have already committed to improving your personal financial situation. Now, it is just a matter of adding more structure, organization, and steps to the process. By the way, this is the fun part because looking at your numbers will allow you to establish a starting point from which to measure your future success.

OBJECTIVES:

1. To understand the difference between savings and emergency funds
2. To understand what portion of your net pay is allocated to various spending categories
3. To understand cash flow planning
4. To understand how to create your debt blitz plan

OUTCOMES:

Upon successful completion of this lesson, you will have a better understanding of:

> How to distinguish between when to use savings versus emergency fund money
> How to give your cash an assignment before you receive it
> How to create and follow a plan to pay off debt

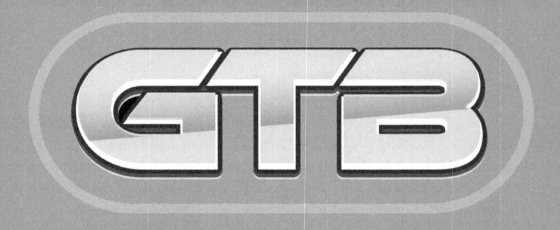

LESSON 11

Savings versus Emergency Funds

Savings — Money set aside for a planned event

Examples: Christmas, vacation, braces, anniversary celebration, birthday

Emergency Fund — Money set aside for unplanned events

Examples: furnace or air conditioning unit stops working, refrigerator in need of repair, plumbing problems, medical emergencies, paying an insurance deductible due to an unforeseen event

You have been reading a lot about savings and emergency funds. To be clear, they are both types of savings accounts. For the purpose of getting on the right financial track, think of them in two different ways even though they are both called "savings accounts."

Savings

Some people may have a savings account, but many people do not have any emergency funds (recall the Bench Warmer exercise). Depending on the situation, when someone has money in a *savings account* (future planned event), it can quickly become an *emergency fund* if that is all the money he has in reserves. The two are very different. Use money from your savings account if you plan to spend funds at a future date (e.g., vacation, braces, landscaping). When something occurs unexpectedly (e.g., car problems, furnace inoperable, refrigerator on the blink) and requires money to get fixed right away, that is an emergency. Sometimes people confuse the two.

If you have been saving money for a vacation but used that money to have your car repaired, your savings ended up being an emergency fund. To best solve this problem, why not have two funds? If you have serious debt challenges, consider only establishing an initial emergency fund of at least $500, $1,000 or $1,500 (Key Play #1 of the Game Time Budgeting system). You may have to delay saving for that vacation until a later date. Remember, it is difficult hitting a goal without some type of sacrifice.

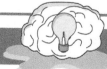

TIP

In an effort to curb your desire to inappropriately access money in your emergency fund, consider opening an account at a financial institution where you do not currently have funds.

LESSON 12

Typical U.S. Household Flow of Money

This diagram represents what some people like to call the debt trap. For most people, payday is a happy experience. Unfortunately, others have come to discover that payday is simply a step in their process of overspending. This sounds odd, but you have to really think about this concept. If you work only to pay debt and lack savings, an emergency fund, and an investment portfolio, this is a continuous journey on the path to nowhere. The only way to break this cycle is to do something different. You may have heard this definition of insanity...doing the same thing over and over and expecting a different result.

From this day forward, please remember there is a consequence for every action you take regarding money. Some consequences are good; some consequences are not so good. The great part is that you have 100% control of your money, so go ahead and tell it what to do.

LESSON 13

Introduction to Creating Spending Plans

It is time to experience one of the most powerful things on earth — creating a spending plan or budget. If you have strange feelings associated with the words *spending plan* or *budget*, relax. You have been misinformed and now will learn how empowering this process can be. A budget is nothing more than a written plan for your money which includes income and expenses for a specific period of time. Isn't it interesting that corporations prepare budgets all the time, but individuals do not like to count their own money? If you are the type that says, "I keep my budget in my head," stop kidding yourself.

Unlike you, some people have a problem of doing the wrong thing over and over. Now that you have fully embraced the Game Time Budgeting system, you are prepared to win. Before we go any further, here are a few tips:

1. Your budget is the final authority or the last word regarding financial decisions. In addition, you have to understand the role emotions play in your finances. You may have heard the saying, "Think with your heart and not your mind." That makes no sense at all. Thinking implies that you are using your brain and that is the end of the story. If you routinely listen to your emotions rather than logic, your financial life will not be any better a year from now than it is today.

2. Whether single or married, you must have a budget review meeting. The best time to have a budget meeting is the last week of the month prior to receiving your next paycheck. For example, if it is the final week of January, you would have your February budget meeting during that week. One of the tricks to budgeting is getting your plan down on paper before the money actually touches your hands or is deposited into your bank account. You probably have a paper or electronic calendar, so go ahead and schedule your budget review meetings for the rest of the year. When you have an appointment written down, it decreases the chances it will be missed.

3. There is always going to be a number of different opinions about your budget. The important part is to reach a final decision. Again, if you are married, do not look at the budget as doing it *your* way or *my* way, it should be done *our* way.

4. If you are married and one person likes taking notes or using spreadsheets, that person can do the data entry. However, the budget should always be done as a couple. As you may have heard before, there is no "I" in team.

5. When you want to make a change in your life, find an accountability partner. Most people fail to accomplish their goals because they do not tell anyone what they plan to achieve. If they told someone, then they would have to put in the work to make that goal a reality. Most of us have at least one good friend (not a yes buddy). Ask that individual to be your accountability partner. All you have to do is tell him or her what to hold you accountable for. Simple, isn't it?

6. The envelope system is very old but easy to execute. After you determine how much money you want to spend on a certain category, you simply place the cash in an envelope and label it accordingly. For example, if you budgeted $50 for entertainment, upon receiving your check, put $50 inside an envelope and write the word "entertainment" on the outside. Use the cash inside this envelope anytime you spend money on entertainment. When the money is gone, the entertainment is over. That's it. Period! The envelope system is best used for categories like entertainment, grocery, eating out, and barber/beauty shop spending.

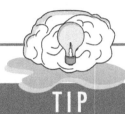

TIP

We live in a world that is quickly becoming a cashless society. If the envelope system is not practical for your life, I am sure you may be able to find an app that could meet your needs. The goal is to master the art of discipline with your money. Whatever method you choose to accomplish this goal is great if you are getting the results you desire.

BUDGETING STEPS

1. Understand **WHY** you are creating a budget
2. Determine net income.
3. Determine expenses.
4. Reduce expenses or generate more income if you need better cash flow. Doing both may be ideal.
5. Determine how to use excess cash flow. Either increase you emergency fund, pay down debt, or build up savings.
6. Spend all income for the month (income minus expenses should equal $0).
7. Periodically review spending (weekly, bi-weekly, monthly).

How much can John B. Free put toward his Emergency Fund?

John is ready to do his spending plan for the following month. The intent of this exercise is to expose you to directing John's income so that he can save, pay his day-to-day bills, and plan for future expenses. Assume John's Garbage/Recycling and Car Insurance bills are not due until 3 and 6 months from now, respectively. There is no right or wrong answer.

Income:	
Monthly Net Income	**$2,900**
Monthly Gross Income	**$4,000**

Non-Monthly Bills:	
Garbage & Recycling	**$60** every 3 months
Car Insurance	**$210** every 6 months

Giving

Emergency Fund

Household/Utilities

Mortgage	$900
Garbage & Recycling	
Utilities	$80
Water	$25
Phone (cell only)	$60
Cable	$0
Groceries	$200

Transportation

Car Payment	$320
Car Insurance	
Gas	

Debts

Student Loan	$150
Credit Card #1	$10
Credit Card #2	$15
Credit Card #3	$50
Credit Card #4	$25

Personal

Entertainment

Clothing

Your Financial Fitness

The assignments for Quarter 3 are listed below. This workbook dedicates considerable time to discussing how your money must be organized if you want to achieve your financial goals. These exercises will give you more understanding of your personal finances than you may think possible. You will use the **Game Time Budgeting electronic cash flow planning tools** to complete the worksheets.

Game Plan — monthly expenses

Assists — recommended expense category percentages

Debt Blitz Exercise — debt reduction/elimination

Debt Blitz — personal form

Recovery Exercise — not enough money to pay minimums

Recovery — personal form

If you have ever wondered what happens to all your money over a month's time, this is your chance to find out. Because your life is so busy, you may not have taken the time to track how much you spend and where your money goes. The **Game Plan** worksheet will help you see, in black and white, where your money is being spent. If you need assistance with these amounts, reference a copy of your last month's bank and credit card statements which detail your spending. Enter the amount you spend on each of the various categories. If there is a category you need but it is missing, simply type in the name of that category and enter the appropriate amount.

The worksheet is designed to automatically total the amounts in each of the respective categories, so you can determine what percentage of your net income is being spent. For example, if you bring home $4,000 per month and spend $1,000 per month on your mortgage, that means you spend 25% ($1,000/$4,000 x 100) of your net income on housing.

While completing this exercise, you may be alarmed to discover you are spending more per month than you bring home. This is not surprising if you have always had the habit of running out of money before the end of the month. To overcome this challenge, all you have to do is determine what items in your monthly expenses can be minimized or eliminated. As you may recall, you spent time in Quarter 1 determining what monthly expenses in your financial household could be reduced or eliminated. Now is the time to put your ideas into action.

To complete the worksheet, follow these simple steps:

1. Enter the **total amount of take-home pay for your household** beside "Total Household Income" at the bottom of the **Game Plan** worksheet.
2. Within each category (Charitable Giving, Housing, etc.), enter the amount of money spent for that respective item during a month.
3. Continue this process for all the categories you use within a month. This worksheet is a little lengthy. It was designed this way so you wouldn't forget something important. Depending on your household's expenses, you may not have to enter a dollar value for every line item.
4. The "Category Total" column is used to sum the expenses within a particular category. When using the electronic worksheets, these calculations are done automatically. As an example, when you add all your individual utilities, the result should go in the box under the "Category Total" column which corresponds with the "Utilities" section. Enter the respective totals in the "Category Total" column.

Now that all your expenses for the month have been captured and summed in the Category Total columns, it's time to determine what percentage of your take-home pay each category represents. To do this, simply divide your total for a particular category by your "Total Household Income" and multiply by 100. This number represents how much of your take-home pay is allocated toward a specific category expressed as a percentage. For example, let's suppose your housing expense for the month is $300 and your total household income is $1,000. Your housing as a percent of take home pay would be 30%. You would calculate your percent of take- home pay like this: ($300/$1,000) x 100 = 30%.

You can compare your percent of take-home pay amounts to the recommended percentages listed on your **Assists** form.

> - If there is an asterisk (*) beside an item, consider using the envelope system.
> - Remember to include items captured on your **Trick Plays** form.
> - "Grand Total" represents the sum of all category totals.
> - "Balance" is determined by subtracting "Total Household Income" from "Grand Total."

Game Plan

Anyone who earns an income and incurs expenses must have a "Game Plan" or "Cash Flow Plan." Every dollar you earn should have a purpose and should be spent using this form. When you deduct your expenses from your income, the amount remaining should be zero. If your balance does not equal zero, that means you have not spent all your income on paper, as required, when doing a cash flow plan. If you have trouble deciding what to do with the extra money, consider allocating more towards debt, savings, or giving.

Your "Cash Flow Planning" can be broken down into various categories. Some of which may include: Giving, Saving, Housing, Utilities, Food, Transportation, Recreation, Medical, Personal, and Debt.

		Category Total	% of Take Home Pay
CHARITABLE GIVING			
SAVING			
Emergency Fund			
Retirement Fund			
College Fund			
HOUSING			
Mortgage Payment			
Homeowner Assoc. Fee			
Homeowner's Insurance			
Repairs or Maint. Fee			
Real Estate Taxes			
UTILITIES			
Electricity			
Water			
Gas			
Bundle: Phone/cable/Internet		If you bundle skip the next three cells	
Phone			
Cable			
Internet			
Garbage and Recycling			
Alarm			
FOOD			
* Groceries & Home Goods			
* Dining Out			
TRANSPORTATION			
Car Payment #1			
Car Payment #2			
Car Payment #3			
* Gas & Oil			
Maintenance			
Insurance			
Tax and Tag			
Public Transportation			
RECREATION			
Gym/fitness			
Vacation			
* Entertainment			
SUB-TOTAL			

		Category Total	% of Take Home Pay
MEDICAL			
Health Insurance		Input Insurance payments if not automatically drafted from paycheck.	
Disability Insurance			
Life Insurance			
Doctor Bills			
Dentist			
Eye Doctor			
Medications			
PERSONAL			
Salon/Barber			
Child Care			
Personal Care			
Tuition			
School Supplies			
Child Support			
Alimony			
Subscriptions			
Gifts			
Club Dues			
Misc. Spending			
Dry Cleaning			
Clothing			
Christmas Saving			
DEBTS (Write in Type)			
Credit Card			
Credit Card			
Credit Card			
Credit Card			
Credit Card			
Credit Card			
Credit Card			
School Loan #1			
School Loan #2			
Other			
Other			
Other			
Other			
SUB-TOTAL			

GRAND TOTAL

TOTAL HOUSEHOLD INCOME — input monthly income here

BALANCE

Recommended
Expense Category Percentages

You will need the **Game Plan** worksheet to complete this exercise. Since you went through the process of determining what percentage of your net income went to each expense category, compare those percentages to the recommended ranges listed on the **Assists** worksheet. As an example, if your net income is $1,000 per month and you spend $400 per month on a car payment, you are spending 40% of your take-home pay on transportation. As seen on the **Assists** worksheet, this amount should be within 10% to 15% of your net income. Obviously, if you earn an unusually high income, you have to use your best judgment regarding the recommended ranges.

Assists occur when one player helps another player score. This form offers suggestions on how much of your "net pay" should be spent on certain expenses. These are only recommendations and may not apply if you have an abnormal income (extremely high or extremely low). For example, if you take home $10,000 a month, you should not spend $1,000 on food. Depending on your current lifestyle, it may be necessary to adjust how your money is allocated to meet your financial goals.

Category	Recommended %	Actual %
Charitable Giving	10 — 15%	
Housing	25 — 30%	
Saving	10 — 15%	
Transportation	10 — 15%	
Utilities	5 — 10%	
Food	5 — 15%	
Clothing	3 — 5%	
Medical/Health	5 — 10%	
Personal	5 — 10%	
Recreation	5 — 10%	
Debts	5 — 10%	

Debt Reduction/Elimination

One of the goals valued most at Game Time Budgeting is helping people become debt-free. To reach this goal, you have to create a plan to eliminate debt and stick to the plan. There are two main theories regarding paying off debt. You can either pay off your debts in order of smallest to largest or pay off your debt in order of highest to lowest interest rate. Because they are more costly, paying off the debt(s) with the highest interest rates makes the most sense. However, the root of your money problems is probably not the inability to do simple math. Game Time Budgeting supports paying off your debts by any means necessary (legal of course). For most people, it is often easier to pay down debts from the smallest to largest balance. Seeing a quick win is motivating when facing an uphill financial journey. If you have individual debts totaling $5,000, $1,000, and $500, you should be able to eliminate the $500 debt with just a little focused intensity. By eliminating the $500 debt quickly, you increase the likelihood of continuing along this path.

Once a debt is paid off, move to the next largest debt. In the above example, it would be the $1,000 debt. Whatever amount of money you were paying on the $500 debt, you now shift that over to the $1,000 debt. This process is repeated over and over until your debts are eliminated. Yes, it's that simple. Don't make this process more difficult than it has to be by saying things like, "I'm tired of living below my means" or "I think I need to treat myself to something new." You're an adult, not a crybaby. Besides, it may have taken you a number of years to get into debt; so naturally, you will not get out of debt overnight.

Debt Blitz Exercise

John B. Free has completed his Game Plan and realized he has money left over. His $1,000 emergency fund is fully funded. His next step is to start working on his Debt Blitz. What is John B. Free's Debt Blitz plan for the next three months? Assume no interest is added to his debt load and the minimum payment amounts have already been included in his Game Plan calculations.

March — Remaining Balance — $150

Debt	Total Payoff Amount	Minimum Payment	New Payment
MasterCard	$200.00	$5.00	
Visa	$300.00	$10.00	
Discover	$750.00	$25.00	
Chase	$1,500.00	$100.00	
Capital One	$2,000.00	$150.00	

April — Remaining Balance — $100

Debt	Total Payoff Amount	Minimum Payment	New Payment
MasterCard	$45.00	$5.00	
Visa	$300.00	$10.00	
Discover	$750.00	$25.00	
Chase	$1,500.00	$100.00	
Capital One	$2,000.00	$150.00	

May — Remaining Balance — $200

Debt	Total Payoff Amount	Minimum Payment	New Payment
MasterCard		$0.00	
Visa	$240.00	$10.00	
Discover	$750.00	$25.00	
Chase	$1,500.00	$100.00	
Capital One	$2,000.00	$150.00	

Debt Blitz

In football, when the defense wants to put pressure on the quarterback in hopes of disrupting a play or causing a turnover, they run a blitz. The Debt Blitz is the most crucial part of getting out of debt. All it requires is a reasonable income, focused intensity, desire, and a plan. In the worksheet below, list your debts (smallest to largest balance) along with related total payoff amounts and minimum payments. The Debt Blitz philosophy requires you to pay the minimum balance on all your debt except the debt with the smallest balance. The idea is to put as much money as possible toward the smallest debt, eliminating it in the shortest amount of time possible. After paying off the smallest debt, move on to the next smallest debt. Again, put as much money as possible toward this debt until it is paid in full. Continue this trend until all your debt has been eliminated. Depending on your income, debt, and intensity level, eliminating your debt can happen as fast or as slow as YOU decide.

The "New Payment" column represents the amount you were paying on the previous debt plus the current debt's minimum payment. As you work through your **Debt Blitz**, the amounts you pay toward eliminating debt should start to increase. The example below shows how money normally spent on a smaller debt is added to the next debt. As you can see, over time, all of the minimum payments previously used to pay the smaller debts are included in the payment for the largest debt. These "New Payment" figures do not consider any additional funds allocated to pay off debt via the **Game Plan** worksheet.

Example

Debt	Total Payoff Amount	Minimum Payment	New Payment
MasterCard	$100.00	$10.00	
Visa	$150.00	$15.00	$25.00
Discover	$500.00	$50.00	$75.00
Chase	$1,000.00	$100.00	$175.00
Capital One	$1,500.00	$150.00	$325.00

Your Debt Blitz

Debt	Total Payoff Amount	Minimum Payment	New Payment

Not Enough Money to Meet Minimum Credit Card Payments

If you ever find yourself in a situation where you have cut your monthly living expenses to the lowest possible amount but still can't meet all the minimum monthly payments due on your credit card debt, you may want to consider using the *Recovery* method. To keep it simple, calculate how much money you have left after taking care of the necessities. After that, determine what percentage of your total debt each bill represents. Let's assume that after completing your budget you only have $300 left to pay debts. Your minimum monthly payments, however, total $400. What do you do now? In the following example, you could give each creditor a fair share of your $300.

List of Credit Cards	Column A Balance	Column B Total Debt	Column C (A/B*100)	Column D $ Available	Column E (C*D)
Credit Card 1	$100	$1,500	6.67%	$300	$20.01
Credit Card 2	$200	$1,500	13.33%	$300	$39.99
Credit Card 3	$300	$1,500	20.00%	$300	$60.00
Credit Card 4	$400	$1,500	26.67%	$300	$80.01
Credit Card 5	$500	$1,500	33.33%	$300	$99.99
Total Debt	**$1,500**		**100%**		**$300.00**

As you can see, you will not be making the minimum payment due on any of your bills. Nevertheless, if you show your creditor that you're making an effort to pay on your debts, I doubt the payment will be refused.

Another method some people opt to use is paying certain debt(s) off in full and making payment on the others later. In the above example, the first two credit cards could be paid off in full with the $300 and the other three debts (cards 3, 4, and 5) would be paid late. If you choose this method, do your research to determine the consequences of your actions. Remember, there is a consequence to every action taken involving money.

One other option is to sell something of value to make up the difference between your minimum payments and cash on hand. This may not excite you, but at least you're making minimum payments.

Recovery

Recovery in football occurs when a team gains or retains possession of a fumbled ball. In terms of your debt blitz, recovery represents regaining control of your debt load. When you don't have enough money to pay the minimum payments on your debt, you have to allocate payments to your creditors based on the amount of your debt they represent. Obviously, you will not be meeting the minimum payments required by your creditors. However, something is better than nothing. If you need to send a copy of your budget to customer service to make your case, consider it.

Example:

Disposable Income		$225.00	Total Minimum Payments		$325.00	
		A	B	C= (A/B) x 100	D	E=C x D
Debt	Minimum Payment Amount	Payoff Amount	Total Debt	Percent	Disposable Income	New Payment
MasterCard	$25.00	$100.00	$3,250.00	3%	$225.00	$6.92
Visa	$50.00	$150.00	$3,250.00	5%	$225.00	$10.38
Discover	$75.00	$500.00	$3,250.00	15%	$225.00	$34.62
Chase	$75.00	$1,000.00	$3,250.00	31%	$225.00	$69.23
Capital One	$100.00	$1,500.00	$3,250.00	46%	$225.00	$103.85
Total	**$325.00**	**$3,250.00**				**$225.00**

Disposable Income			Total Minimum Payments			
		A	B	C= (A/B) x 100	D	E=C x D
Debt	Minimum Payment Amount	Payoff Amount	Total Debt	Percent	Disposable Income	New Payment
Total						

1. Determine if you need a recovery plan:

   a. Referencing the **Bench Warmer** worksheet, subtract the amount in the "Total Monthly Necessities" field from your monthly income. This is your "Disposable Income" for this exercise.

   b. Referencing the **Personal Fouls** worksheet, enter the Minimum Payment Amount for each credit card. Sum the total minimum credit card payments due (automatically calculated in the worksheet). This is your "Total Minimum Payments" amount.

   c. If your disposable income is less than the minimum payments, a recovery plan is needed. Remember, your disposable income represents the amount of money which will be distributed among your creditors according to the percentage of your total debt they represent.

2. Enter the Payoff Amounts for each credit card from the **Personal Fouls** worksheet. Sum the payoff amounts to determine the Total Debt (automatically calculated in this spreadsheet).

3. Now divide each payoff amount by the Total Debt figure. This number represents the percentage of that respective debt as compared to your total debt.

4. Next, multiply the appropriate percent times your disposable income referenced in step 1. This New Payment represents the amount of money to send to that respective creditor.

Recovery Exercise

John B. Free found out he now has to pay child support. His monthly Game Plan balance will not cover his minimum monthly credit card payments. John decided to pay off the remaining $25 balance on his Visa and plan a "Recovery" for his remaining debt. Help John work his Recovery plan.

Disposable Income: $200.00

Debt	Total Payoff Amount	Total Debt	Percent	Disposable Income	New Payment
MasterCard	Paid Off				
Visa	Paid Off				
Discover	$ 750.00				
Chase	$ 1,500.00				
Capital One	$ 2,500.00				
Total					

QUARTER 4

It's GAME TIME!

COURSE DESCRIPTION:

Everyone earning an income needs to create and implement one of the most important financial systems — a budget. This course will equip you with the necessary tools to make your money behave once and for all (That's my hope!).

OBJECTIVES:

1. To provide a planning guide on how to allocate your financial resources for an entire month
2. To provide a tracking mechanism for comparing projected spend versus actual spending

OUTCOMES:

Upon successful completion of this lesson, you will have a better understanding of:

> How to create and implement an efficient monthly spending plan
> How to use your budget as a guide to determine your financial possibilities

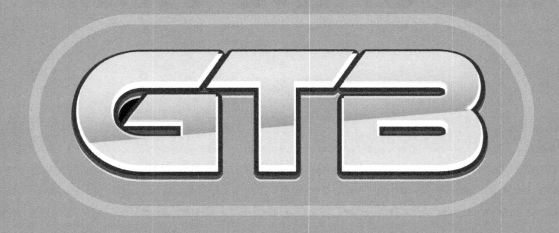

LESSON 14

Cash Flow Planning

Cash flow planning in its simplest form means dictating to your cash how it should behave. Money does not have a brain, but it has the ability to act like a well-trained animal. It will do exactly what you tell it to do. If you command it to be wasteful, it will. If you command it to be on good behavior, it will. You work very hard for your money, so do yourself a favor and give it the respect it deserves.

The coaching you have been exposed to throughout this entire workbook has been leading up to the big game. You could very well say that this is a championship matchup. It's you versus your debt and day-to-day financial choices. We already know who's going to win. If you have a trophy around the house, go ahead and make your victory acceptance speech.

You have invested a considerable amount of time training your mind and learning the three key plays. The only thing left to do is play the game. You guessed it. **It's Game Time!**

The assignments for Quarter 4 are listed below. The previous lessons have prepared you for this moment. Using these worksheets each month can help you better track income and expenses. They can also serve as a guide toward increasing savings or eliminating debt. You will use the **Game Time Budgeting electronic cash flow planning tools** to complete the worksheets.

Game Time — allocate net income to pay periods

Stats — budgeted amount versus actual spend

The **Game Time** worksheet allows you to allocate your net income specific to each pay period. The goal is to "spend" all your income on paper or electronically before you receive it. By doing this, your money already has purpose, direction, and an assignment.

The **Game Time** worksheet is very detailed which may cause you to feel a little anxious. Remember to keep it simple. Only think about one line item at a time. Each expense that is entered will be subtracted from your income. The entire worksheet is a summary of income and expenses. When you think about it, it's only addition and subtraction. This may be your first time ever trying to put together a spending plan or budget. Remember, the first time you do anything is the most challenging. The more you do something, the easier it gets. You can do it!

If you are new to this process, insert an amount for uncategorized spending. That does not mean inserting a number like $500; amounts like $25 or $50 are more appropriate. Uncategorized spending represents an unforeseen error in the budgeting process. Once you get the hang of it, you will be able to eliminate this category all together because you will have mastered the **Game Time** worksheet.

If you are the type of person who gets excited about new things and says, "I'll give it a try," here's a newsflash. The word *try* implies that failure is an option. Either you're going to do it or you are not. Those are the only two choices.

You now have all the tools you need to accomplish your goal of becoming debt-free and/or creating a more stable monthly financial plan. The only thing left to do is repeat this process over and over every month for the rest of your life. Even after you become debt-free, you still have to give your money an assignment so it will not misbehave.

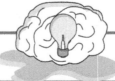

TIP

Consider creating an e-mail account strictly for your money (e.g., MrAlsBills@gmail.com). This will help with organizing your financial documents so nothing gets lost. Don't forget to update your various accounts with the new email address so everything is sent to the right place.

The **Game Time** worksheet allows you to spend, on paper or electronically all your money for each pay period of a month in a few simple steps. This worksheet should capture all household income and expenses; therefore, married couples need to complete this form together.

1. Under the "Pay Period" columns, enter your pay dates for the month. Depending on how often you are paid, all of these columns may not be used. Be sure to include pay dates for both spouses if you are married.

2. Locate the "INCOME" row on the worksheet. Move across the row and enter your net income in the white box of each pay period for which a paycheck is received. If you and your spouse receive paychecks during the same week, enter your combined income amounts in the white box so the funds can be allocated accordingly.

3. Note the list of expenses on the left side of the worksheet. Each expense has a white box which corresponds to a particular pay period. You will need to assign each expense to the appropriate pay period(s). It may help to reference your bill due dates which were captured on the **Starting Line** worksheet. Record the amount you plan to pay on a bill or expense in the white box which matches the applicable pay period. Once you enter an amount, subtract that number from that pay period's income amount and place the result in the gray box beside that expense (automatically calculated in the spreadsheet). Each time you enter a new expense amount, subtract this figure from the previous gray box amount and enter the result beside the new expense. Please note, your income total will continue to decrease each time you spend money on a bill or allocate funds in other categories. Be mindful that some bills are paid monthly like your water bill, and other bills may be paid weekly like your grocery bill, so plan accordingly. Allocating your income to bills at the beginning of the month allows you to be more prepared for the future.

4. Your goal for each paycheck is to spend all the money on paper or electronically so your last gray box figure is zero ($0). If you use the **electronic cash flow planning tools**, your "Amt. Left" at the top of each pay period should equal $0.00. Having a zero balance simply means you have told your money how to behave during a respective pay period.

Game Time!

This worksheet allows you to spend all of your money on paper or electronically before each pay period. Each column represents a pay period. Depending on how often you get paid, some of these columns may not be used. Married couples need to complete this form together. Enter your combined net income amounts during weeks where you both get paid.

	Pay Period 1		Pay Period 2		Pay Period 3		Pay Period 4		Pay Period 5	
Date										
	Amt. Left:		Amt. Left:		Amt. Left:		Amt. Left:		Amt. Left:	
INCOME										
EXPENSES										
CHARITABLE GIVING										
SAVING										
Regular Savings										
Emergency Fund										
Retirement Fund										
College Fund										
HOUSING										
Mortgage Payment										
Homeowner Assoc. Fee										
Homeowner's Insurance										
Repairs or Maint. Fee										
Real Estate Taxes										
UTILITIES										
Electricity										
Water										
Gas										
Phone/Cable/Internet										
Phone										
Cable										
Internet										
Garbage and Recycling										
Alarm										
FOOD										
*Groceries/Home Goods										
*Dining Out										
TRANSPORTATION										
Car Payment #1										
Car Payment #2										
Car Payment #3										
*Gas & Oil										
Maintenance										
Insurance										

Tax and Tag									
Public Transportation									

RECREATION

Gym/fitness									
Vacation									
*Entertainment									

MEDICAL

Health Insurance									
Disability Insurance									
Life Insurance									
Doctor Bills									
Dentist									
Eye Doctor									
Medications									

PERSONAL

*Salon/Barber									
Child Care									
Personal Care									
Tuition									
School Supplies									
Child Support									
Alimony									
Subscriptions									
Gifts									
Club Dues									
*Misc. Spending									
*Dry Cleaning									
Clothing									
Christmas Saving									

DEBTS (Write in Type)

Credit Card									
Credit Card									
Credit Card									
Credit Card									
Credit Card									
Credit Card									
Credit Card									
School Loan #1									
School Loan #2									
Other									
Other									
Other									
Other									

Budgeted Amount
minus Actual Spend

A player's stats or statistics show how well he performs during GAME TIME. This worksheet will help you determine how close you are to meeting the actual budgeted amounts for a respective category within a month.

The expense categories on the left should be an exact duplication of the categories used in the **Game Time** worksheet. The "Budget from (GAME TIME)" column is a sum total of the allocated amounts in each pay period of the **Game Time** worksheet. Enter the actual expense of a category in the "Actual Spending" column. To determine how close you came to hitting your budgeted amount, subtract the "Actual Spending" total from the "Budget from (GAME TIME)" amount. Enter the result in the "Difference" column (automatically calculated in the worksheet).

If your overall difference is positive and you have extra money at the end of the month, apply these remaining funds to the next month's smallest debt.

Stats

A player's stats show how well he performs during GAME TIME. This worksheet will help you determine how close you are to meeting the actual budgeted amounts for a respective category within a month. The expense categories on the left should be an exact duplication of the categories used in the **Game Time** worksheet. The "Budget from (Game Time)" column is a sum total of the allocated amounts in each pay period of the **Game Time** worksheet. Enter the actual expense of a category in the "Actual Spending" column. The difference between the "Actual Spending" total and the "Budget from (GAME TIME)" will show you how close you came to hitting your budgeted amount.

	Budget from (GAME TIME)	Actual Spending	Difference
INCOME			
EXPENSES			
CHARITABLE GIVING			
SAVING			
Regular Savings			
Emergency Fund			
Retirement Fund			
College Fund			
HOUSING			
Mortgage Payment			
Homeowner Assoc. Fee			
Homeowner's Insurance			
Repairs or Maintenance Fee			
Real Estate Taxes			
UTILITIES			
Electricity			
Water			
Gas			
Phone/cable/Internet			
Phone			
Cable			
Internet			
Garbage and Recycling			
Alarm			
FOOD			
*Groceries/Home Goods			
*Dining Out			
TRANSPORTATION			
Car Payment #1			
Car Payment #2			
Car Payment #3			
*Gas & Oil			
Maintenance			
Insurance			
Tax and Tag			
Public Transportation			

	Budget from (GAME TIME)	Actual Spending	Difference
RECREATION			
Gym/fitness			
Vacation			
*Entertainment			
MEDICAL			
Health Insurance			
Disability Insurance			
Life Insurance			
Doctor Bills			
Dentist			
Eye Doctor			
Medications			
PERSONAL			
Salon/Barber			
Child Care			
Personal Care			
Tuition			
School Supplies			
Child Support			
Alimony			
Subscriptions			
Gifts			
Club Dues			
Misc. Spending			
Dry Cleaning			
Clothing			
Christmas Saving			
DEBTS (Write in Type)			
Credit Card			
Credit Card			
Credit Card			
Credit Card			
Credit Card			
Credit Card			
Credit Card			
School Loan #1			
School Loan #2			
Other			
Other			
Other			
Other			

Now What?

- ⊙ Celebrate (cash only)

- ⊙ Continue to live below your means

- ⊙ Plan for the future

- ⊙ Continue to save

- ⊙ Give more

AUTOMATIC CALENDAR ALERTS

JANUARY
▸ Final week — Prepare budget for next month
▸ Determine financial goals and create plan for the year

FEBRUARY
▸ Prepare for taxes — filing deadline in April
▸ Final week — Prepare budget for next month

MARCH
▸ File taxes
▸ Final week — Prepare budget for next month

APRIL
▸ Final week — Prepare budget for next month
▸ Check your credit reports (TransUnion, Equifax, and Experian) to review for errors and check your credit score

MAY
▸ Final week — Prepare budget for next month
▸ Review insurance policies and adjust accordingly for life changes (i.e., Big three: marriage, new child, divorce)

JUNE
▸ Final week — Prepare budget for next month
▸ **Midyear:** Compare projected versus actual goal achievement for yearly financial plan

JULY
▸ Final week — Prepare budget for next month

AUGUST
▸ Final week — Prepare budget for next month

SEPTEMBER
▸ Final week — Prepare budget for next month

OCTOBER
▸ Final week — Prepare budget for next month
▸ Annual open enrollment on your job should be approaching. Consider increasing your savings rate.

NOVEMBER
▸ Final week — Prepare budget for next month

DECEMBER
▸ Start saving now for next year's holiday season
▸ Final week — Prepare budget for next month
▸ End of year financial plan review

When you were younger, you may have had many different dreams about what you wanted to do when you became an adult. As you grew into adulthood, you may have allowed someone to discourage you from achieving your dreams. This is what happens to most people as a result of listening to and believing negative outside influences. Just because you age, is that a reason to place limits on your abilities? If something hasn't been done, does that mean you can't do it? If everyone in your family has always had money problems, why not become the first person in your family to break the cycle?

Many people in your life may not agree with your new attitude regarding money and the sacrifices you are making to achieve your goals. Don't worry about what other people say. You have to live your best life, not the life somebody else wants you to live. People will always have an opinion. While everyone else is busy giving their opinions, you should be busy getting results. Your financial dreams and goals are yours. Don't give anyone the power to steal your dream.

Thank you for giving Game Time Budgeting the opportunity to assist in helping you unleash tomorrow's possibilities.

To Your Financial Fitness!

Al Riddick

Al Riddick, President

P.S. — We would love to hear your success stories. Please post them at:

www.GameTimeBudgeting.com

Also by Alfred D. Riddick, Jr.

Challenge, **Educate**, and **Equip** today's youth to enhance their financial fitness. This workbook makes learning about money fun and exciting through a variety of exercises that are:

▶ Engaging

▶ Educational

▶ Entertaining

▶ Real-world financial scenarios

▶ Thought-provoking

⊙ Ideal for classroom or small group

⊙ Facilitator's Guide available

Contact **www.GameTimeBudgeting.com** to inquire about bulk order discounts!

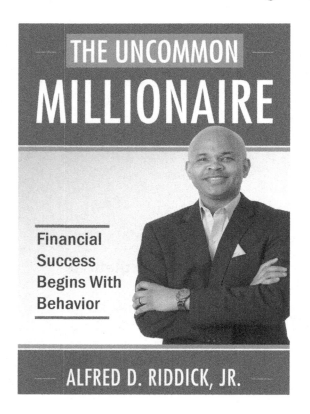

The Uncommon Millionaire reveals a small-town boy's journey from the North Carolina tobacco fields to achieving millionaire status in his late 30's. Al's common-sense approach is mixed with humor accompanied by personal stories of financial challenge and triumph. His story captures your attention and prompts you to maximize your financial potential. Reading this book will help you understand how simple it is to take control of your financial life and create the outcomes you desire.

Made in the USA
Las Vegas, NV
07 February 2021